LOOK
LEAD
LOVE
LEARN

**Four steps to better business,
a better life—and conquering
complexity in the process**

BILL SHERIDAN

Voxie
MEDIA

Look, Lead, Love, Learn
Four steps to better business, a better life—and conquering complexity in the process

Copyright © 2014 by Bill Sheridan
All rights reserved

Published by **Voxie Media**
Big Ideas. Short Books.™
voxiemedia.com

ISBN 978-0-9886203-7-7
eISBN 978-0-9886203-8-4

Printed in the United States of America
Updated edition, 2014

Cover and interior design: Vook and 1106 Design
Copyediting: Barbara McNichol
Proofreading: April Rondeau

CONTENTS

This is a book about navigating a world of rapid change and increasing complexity. It's a book about leadership in a time when we need more leaders at all levels. It's also a book about love. Yes, love—that essential ingredient that creates engagement, inspiration, and the emotional connections that are more important than ever in our always-on, digital, ADD world. Love is the glue that holds our organizations, families, and friends together.

Think of it as a user's guide to the "new normal," a handy reference for that perfect inspirational passage just when you need it. *Look, Lead, Love, Learn* takes you on a world tour of the business and accounting profession. Bill visits the top meetings and conventions and interviews the leading business thinkers in the world, such as Dan Burrus, Andrew Zolli, Rita McGrath, Emmanuel

Gobillot, Brian Solis, Peter Sheahan, and many more. You'll learn the latest in strategic thinking, future trends, leadership, and how to anticipate the fast-arriving future. Aren't we all looking for that edge, that slight advantage that will increase our odds of success?

This book gives you that edge. It's like having the executive summaries of the top 20 business books today, plus the added perspective of young professionals, leaders in the CPA profession, Bill's family and his friends, as well as his wonderful perspective.

I am proud to call Bill a friend and colleague. He is a journalist and reporter who has been covering the CPA profession and the broader world of business for the past 14 years as chief communications officer for the Maryland Association of CPAs and the Business Learning Institute. This book features highlights from our blog, CPASuccess.com, including excerpts and interviews with some of the leading thinkers in the world of business and the accounting profession. It is chock full of wisdom and perspective that will help you shape your own point of view. It will help prepare you for what lies ahead and around the corner and help you see those "weak signals of disruptive change."

This is the kind of book you'll want easy access to. It is a quick read you can dip into when you need special inspiration for that certain situation at work.

I recommend you buy one for your Kindle, your night stand, your backpack, and your desk at work. Send copies to your friends and business colleagues. And don't forget to try the periwinkles.

Tom Hood, CPA, CITP, CGMA
CEO, Maryland Association of CPAs
Business Learning Institute

Shaking the Windows and Rattling the Walls

You better start swimmin'
Or you'll sink like a stone.
— Bob Dylan

Change is a funny thing.

We're used to it being slow, almost imperceptible. Think continental drift or Niagara Falls erosion. You don't know it's happening, but add time and a little time-lapse photography to the mix and you start to see some remarkable things—things that redefine your current reality. Your world is what it is because change and time march on.

And lord, they're marching mighty fast these days.

An educational panel at the Aspen Institute has estimated that, as it relates to science and technology, the rate of change during the next decade is likely to be four to seven times faster than in the previous decade.

Let's put that in perspective. If the rate of change is four times faster, that would be like planning for today in 1890. And if it's seven times faster? That would be like planning for today in *1670*.

We don't need time-lapse photography to see change happen anymore. It's happening all around us—happening, in fact, *to* us—at a nearly constant rate.

Talk about the ultimate paradox: *The only constant today is change.* So if we want to stay relevant, we need to change as well.

When we launched the CPA Success blog six years ago, MACPA Executive Director Tom Hood and I wanted to start a conversation about CPAs' expanding role as trusted business advisors. To a large extent, this blog has accomplished exactly that.

But something happened along the way. The blog's mission changed.

It had to. The world became a much more complex place, and our members felt the stress that always rides shotgun with massive change. CPA Success became a place where Tom and I could shift the conversation to issues that were complicating our members' lives—the changing face of leadership, the growing importance of lifelong learning, the generational differences, the game-changing potential of social media, and, yes, the occasional (and by "occasional" I mean "constant") legislative or regulatory changes that affect this profession.

Along the way, we learned a thing or two as well.

Look, Lead, Love, Learn is a collection of just a few of those lessons.

We've combed the pages of CPA Success for some of our most inspirational and educational posts from the past six years. The teachers featured here are our members, co-workers, families, friends, trusted colleagues, and some of the world's top thought leaders. They're brilliant and inspiring, and we hope you'll learn as much reading the pages that follow as we did writing them.

Tom has created this brilliant formula for conquering complexity:

$$L > C$$

That is, your rate of learning must be greater than the rate of change.

My hope is that this book will boost your L, even if it's just *that* much—a tiny bit. Keep reading and keep learning.

Bill Sheridan

CHAPTER 1

LOOK

We're busier than ever trying to solve today's problems, but the key to overcoming change and complexity is not our reaction to what's happening today. Rather, it's our ability to see what's **going to happen** tomorrow. Plenty of opportunities loom on the horizon—if we take time to come up for air and look for them.

Here are a few tales about the rewards of looking ahead . . . and the perils of looking away.

Innovation is everyone's business.

Think of innovation and you're likely to conjure up images of corporate rock stars, must-have gadgets, or soon-to-be-clichéd thought leadership tracts.

Rock the boat with something new and exciting—
that's innovation, right?

Wrong.

Real innovation, said Andrew Zolli, is less about producing something new and more about anticipating *what's going to be* new—and we *all* can do that.

Zolli, a futurist and CEO of the annual (and highly influential) Pop!Tech Conference as well as a National Geographic Society fellow, has this message: *Anyone* can innovate.

In his keynote address at the conference, he backed up that notion with a pair of definitions:

- "Innovation is the creation of new forms of value in anticipation of future demand."

- And great leaders? They're the ones who systematically scan the horizon for "weak signals of disruptive change." Detecting those signals early and acting on them is key.

After his presentation, I cornered Zolli and asked him to elaborate.

"Our normal metaphors about innovation are all about breakthroughs, change, things that are different, a radical reframing of an industry," he said. "The reality is that most innovative work is incremental improvement. It's about staying ahead of trends as opposed to reacting to trends.

"The challenge is that once you fall behind those trends, a bunker mentality can set in. At that point, you encounter an issue that I call 'cognitive similarity'—people thinking the same way and making that bunker mentality worse.

"We need to engage the very top levels of the organization in a conversation about embracing a different kind of risk portfolio. That means having an established set of processes in place in which *you have no expectation of return*. You make investments not only for operational excellence but for learning and adaptation. Those things are inherently uncertain, but if you do them at a small or medium scale, they can yield tremendous benefits. The cultural changes engendered are significant."

I see a lot of social media's influence in that response. For those focused on traditional ROI metrics, the immediate return on that investment might not be clear, but we have to make the investment nonetheless. Why? In anticipation of *future* returns. Our future students, members, employees, and clients are collaborating via social media. What's the cost if we don't join them?

Now, apply that thinking to *everything* we do. In times of great change, we have to be able to learn new skills, walk new paths, and see what others don't.

Take technology, for example. Groundbreaking technological changes are making data- and information-management services obsolete. That leaves CPAs with the golden opportunity to use their knowledge and wisdom to provide clients with insight, foresight, and consultative value.

"Before I had access to the data and the information, I needed (CPAs) to give it to me," best-selling author Daniel Burrus told the crowd at the 2012 Commerce Clearing House User Conference. "Now, we're heading toward real-time accounting and auditing. When we get to that point, your value shifts to knowledge and wisdom. I need *consultative* value from you—and by the way, I'll pay more for that.

"I need you, but I don't need the *old* you. I need a *new* you who understands the transformation I'm going through as your customer. If you don't, you're out of touch."

And stop thinking you have to keep up with change. "Keeping up is a fool's game," Burrus said.

"I want advantage. I want to do what others aren't doing. I want to see what others aren't seeing."

And that's Zolli's point. His underlying message is this: If you want to *stay* ahead, you have to *look* ahead.

You'll never guess the skill all future leaders need. If you do, you're a future leader yourself.

"Our job," says American Society of Association Executives tech chief Reggie Henry, "is to make the future comfortable for others."

We couldn't agree more.

The idea is this: Leaders need to be early explorers of new frontiers, then help guide their clients there as well.

It's not a new idea. That notion has been bouncing around the thought leadership room for a while now.

- As I mentioned earlier, futurist Andrew Zolli says detecting "weak signals" of disruptive change and acting on them early is the key to future-focused leadership.

- "I need you," futurist Daniel Burrus tells CPAs, "but I don't need the old you. I need a new you who understands the transformation I'm going through as your customer. If you don't, you're out of touch."

- Change management expert Rita McGrath talks about the importance of "deft resource allocation"—knowing when to shift resources from core initiatives to new, more innovative ones.

- In *The Second Machine Age,* authors Erik Brynjolfsson and Andrew McAfee tell us that keeping up is an exercise in futility. If you're just keeping up, that means someone else is always ahead of you.

- "Embrace change," renowned entrepreneur Richard Branson writes simply, "or become stagnant."

A lot of great theories there. Thankfully, though, today we have more than theories—we have definitive proof that it pays to take a proactive, future-focused approach.

According to a survey by The Sleeter Group, 72 percent of small business owners have switched CPAs or accounting firms in part because they believe their CPAs are too reactive and do not provide enough proactive services and advice. In fact, according to the survey, that's the top reason business owners give for leaving their CPAs.

"This reinforces how (small- and mid-size businesses) view the relationship with their accountant," the report states. "They see the CPA as a resource with the knowledge and expertise to help make their business successful, but if the CPA isn't ahead of any potential issues or recommending ways to streamline operations, then the SMB may move on to an accountant who will. It's a good reason for CPAs to make sure they're current on the latest technology solutions for businesses and inform their clients on the benefits."

Daniel Burrus might call that being "anticipatory."

"When you're anticipatory," Burrus writes, "you can not only see and accurately anticipate disruptive technologies, but you can use them to create new revenue streams, new products, new services, and new markets. That's when you drive growth and change from the inside-out so that others have to react to you instead of you reacting to what others are doing. In this scenario, disruption is your friend."

That's another thing we talk a lot about here at the MACPA—the top skills needed for future growth.

Sounds like it's time to add "anticipation" to that list.

Curiosity doesn't kill—it saves.

Want to know the secret of life? The key to absolutely freakin' everything?

I'm not going to tell you.

I'm going to let Andrew Rose, the marketing genius at Baltimore-based CPA firm Naden Lean, tell you instead.

Are you ready? Here it is:

"I'm abundantly curious," Rose said.

That's it. Those three words will unlock everything.

Rose was talking about social media at the time; it was part of a virtual presentation he gave recently to a group of state CPA society communicators in New York City.

And he's right. That's how you conquer social media. Play around with every new social tool on the market. Figure out if it has any value for you and your clients. Ask, "What can it do for me?" Get curious. If you dismiss these social tools—any of them—you'll spend the rest of your life playing catch-up.

But this goes way beyond social media.

Curiosity is how we serve our clients—by asking them about their problems and figuring out ways to solve them.

Curiosity is how we stay ahead of the pace change—by out-learning it. By asking ourselves, "What do I need to do to stay relevant in an increasingly complex world?"

Curiosity is how we stay a step ahead of the competition. The most important skill we'll possess going forward is the ability to learn new skills. Are you learning more than your competitors?

Curiosity is how we grow—by asking questions. By challenging assumptions. By questioning authority. "We've always done it that way" doesn't cut it anymore. "WHY have we always done it that way?" is a great place to start.

What are you curious about? When you know the answer to that question, your future will start to take shape.

If your team isn't doing these six things, you're doomed.

How often do you get a chance to hear one of the world's most influential business thinkers tell you how to conquer change and complexity?

Answer: Not very often.

And yet there she was, Rita McGrath, live in Baltimore, telling a select group of MACPA members how to succeed, even while everything they hold sacred is crumbling around them.

McGrath is a regular at CPA Success. This time around, she focused on what she calls "the end of competitive advantage."

You know those things that set you apart from your competition? They don't set you apart anymore. Everyone has access to the technology, the resources, the data and intelligence that make your offerings unique. And they're probably offering them more cheaply than you are.

So what now?

Time for a reboot.

McGrath offered "a new playbook for strategy"—six rules for how we can stop spinning our wheels and start embracing innovation, collaboration, and new ways of thinking that will truly set us apart. Those who want to succeed going forward, she said, must embrace the following:

1. Continuous reconfiguration: Small changes and new ideas that build on each other can bring substantial payback over time. Organizations that learn to make small but continuous improvements will slowly pull away from the pack.

2. Healthy disengagement: The things that once brought us success will eventually hinder our ability to move forward. Knowing when to shut those things down is important, but that's just the start. Examining what worked, what didn't, and what lessons we can apply to new initiatives will help us move forward more easily.

3. Deft resource allocation: Knowing when to shift resources from core initiatives to new ones—and which resources to shift—will be key as we fill our pipeline with the ideas that will become our new competitive advantages.

4. Innovation proficiency: Innovation itself must become part of our core. How's that for a paradox? But it can't be left to chance. It has to be supported by management, resources, and processes. As Tom Hood tweeted, "The problem is not finding good ideas; it's making innovation systematic."

5. A new leadership mindset: Today's leaders must be discovery-driven, team-building collaborators. They also must be willing to seek out bad news and act on it in a healthy way. "We have the brainpower to solve hard problems," McGrath said, "but we need to recognize those problems first."

6. Entrepreneurial career management: Want to stay relevant to your employer and clients? Start by taking responsibility for your own career. That means constant self-improvement. Learn as much as you can from as many people as you can. Then learn some more.

In short, look forward, not back. Start seizing new opportunities. Spend less time and fewer resources defending your current competitive advantage. And start now.

It won't be a competitive advantage for long.

Stop keeping up. Start setting the pace.

You've heard of Moore's Law, right?

It's the 1965 estimate by Intel co-founder Gordon Moore that computing power will double every 18 months to two years, and it's the framework for the book *The Second Machine Age: Work, Progress, and Prosperity in a Time of Brilliant Technologies,* by Erik Brynjolfsson and Andrew McAfee. Moore initially predicted that his estimate would hold true for about 10 years. He was off by about four decades. It holds true to this day, and it's the reason why the world is as chaotic and complex as it is.

Fifteen years ago, how many of us could have wrapped our brains around concepts like Siri, or Google Glass, or driverless cars? Today's iPhones are as powerful as Apple's top-of-the-line laptops were 10 years ago. The latest iPad is faster than the world's most powerful supercomputer was in 1985. Thinking about stuff like that makes me dizzy, so I'm pretty sure that whatever comes next will make my head explode.

It will also turn each of our jobs upside down. Need proof? Ask a journalist or a recording industry executive, or whoever's in charge of the U.S. Postal Service. The day will come, I swear to God, when filing a tax return—any tax return—will be a completely automated process. What will happen to tax-pro CPAs when that day arrives?

If they're smart, they're not waiting to find out. They're figuring out right now how to add new value to their clients' lives once their traditional services have become outdated and automated. If you're not doing that future-focused work, you're putting yourself at risk of irrelevancy at best . . . and extinction at worst.

In *The Second Machine Age*, Intel executive Mike Marberry is quoted as follows: "If you're only using the same technology, then in principle you run into limits."

That's putting it mildly. If you're only using the same technology, you're a dinosaur.

We talk extensively about "keeping up" with the latest trends, but what good is that? I had this discussion with Jason Blumer and Greg Kyte as part of the Thriveal CPA Network's "Thrivecast," and we all reached pretty much the same conclusion: Keeping up is an exercise in futility. If you're just keeping up, that means someone else is always ahead of you. If your only goal is to keep up with things like social media, mobile technologies, cloud computing, and Big Data, what's your plan for the day when they evolve into The Next Big Thing?

Stop keeping up. Start setting the pace. Make sure you're building in time to look to the horizon and scan for the weak signals of disruptive change.

I don't care what you do for a living—technology is now the foundation upon which you do it. And that foundation is constantly changing.

Change with it, or everything you've built will crumble.

The key to the future? Imagination trumps logic.

We've spent years at CPA Success trying to explain the importance of being ahead of the curve. We could fill a book with what we've written on the subject.

In fact, we have.

Leave it to Reggie Henry to boil that message down to one simple, brilliant thought.

Reggie is a technology god at the American Society of Association Executives—in essence, the association for associations. He snuck into a recent meeting of the Maryland Association of CPAs directors and staff and delivered this call to arms:

"Our job," he said, "is to make the future comfortable for others."

So what does that mean?

In short, it means being a pioneer. It means trying new things before anyone else does, figuring out which of the new stuff is valuable, and sharing it with our stakeholders.

It means being really uncomfortable while we figure out this new stuff, then making our clients comfortable in their ability to use it.

It means always being on the edge, scanning the horizon for the next big thing so our clients don't have to.

It means paving the way for those who follow us.

Imagine how valuable you'll be to your clients if you can do that heavy lifting for them.

It's not easy. It takes hard work, leadership, foresight, and imagination—the ability to see not only the future but also what we need to do to succeed there. The key is to think like your clients. Understand their problems, then imagine how these new trends and tools will help them solve those problems.

"Logic will take you from A to B," Reggie told us, channeling Albert Einstein, "but imagination will take you everywhere."

Time to haul our imaginations out of mothballs, folks. In an era of great change and complexity, imagining our future is the first step toward getting there.

Trouble's brewing. Pay attention.

What happens when you fail to look ahead—when you fail to detect those "weak signals of disruptive change"?

By way of example, the folks at Anheuser-Busch could tell you.

In *Dethroning the King: The Hostile Takeover of Anheuser-Busch,* Julie MacIntosh, a *Financial Times* reporter, examined the internal culture and politics that led to the brewing icon's 2008 takeover at the hands of Belgian/Brazilian beer-making giant InBev.

Anheuser-Busch, of course, is best known as the maker of Budweiser. The company was an American corporate giant. At one point, it controlled 52 percent of the U.S. beer market and owned one of the most iconic and beloved American brands out there.

And that, wrote MacIntosh, was part of the problem. For years, Anheuser-Busch CEO August Busch III was focused solely on crushing rival Miller and dominating the American beer market. He was *so* focused on that one goal, in fact, that he failed to ask this simple question: What happens next?

The answer would be found beyond American borders. One of Busch's fatal flaws was failing to pay enough attention to beer's expanding *global* market. As America's beer-making Goliath, he didn't really need to, right?

But his rivals paid plenty of attention to the global market, buying or merging with foreign beer makers and gobbling up sizeable pieces of the international pie. By the time A-B noticed what was happening, it found itself shut out of the M&A (mergers and acquisitions) action—and ripe for a takeover.

It's an amazing story, really—how a singularly American brand suddenly found itself under foreign control. In St. Louis, a city defined in many ways by its connection to Anheuser-Busch, it's also a heartbreaking tale.

Remember what Andrew Zolli said about innovation? It's about *staying ahead of* trends, not *reacting to* trends.

That's a lesson Anheuser-Busch learned too late, as evidenced by its new name: Anheuser-Busch InBev.

How are *you* monitoring those "weak signals of disruptive change" that affect you?

Change is constant. Action should be, too.

Still, we can't spend all of our time looking ahead, can we? We have a desk full of problems to deal with right now.

The only constant these days is change. That's as clichéd as it gets, but it's true. The economy, the markets, legislation, regulation, communication, technology—they're all conspiring to make our world a living hell, and they're doing it over and over and over again.

So how do we deal with current change?

Peter Sheahan has a few ideas.

Sheahan is the acclaimed author of *Flip: How to Turn Everything You Know on Its Head—and Succeed Beyond Your Wildest Imaginings* and *Making*

It Happen: Turning Good Ideas Into Great Results. As CEO of ChangeLabs, he's a known thought leader in behavioral change and innovation. He believes *action and innovation* will do more to help us conquer change than anything else.

Here are just a few of Sheahan's nuggets of wisdom, excerpted from his keynote address at the 2012 American Society of Association Executive's Annual Meeting in St. Louis:

- Our job going forward is simple . . . and supremely complex. Question all of our assumptions about what's happening now and what it might look like tomorrow. Those assumptions will almost surely be wrong.

- Are you a steward of the past or a driver of change? Are you beholden to clients, members, or employees who are stuck in yesterday, or are you committed to leading people into a brave new world? If you're the former, you'd better figure out how to become the latter.

- The hardest thing about staying awesome is the gravity of success. The more we succeed, the more we want to keep doing the same old things. In a world of change, that's a mistake.

- Complexity breeds specialization, and specialization breeds silos, and silos stifle communication, collaboration, and innovation. We've tried for years now to tear down silos, yet we find ourselves in an era that promotes the very creation of silos. Walls destroy innovation and collaboration. Walls destroy our efforts to outpace the rate of change. Proceed with caution.

- In times of great change, action must come before clarity. We don't have the luxury of examinations, studies, task forces, and white papers. We need to act—and fast. Don't wait for a blueprint. We're building the blueprint on the fly. Take a leap of faith and adjust things after the fact.

I'd add one more suggestion: *Never stop learning.* CPAs are struggling to keep pace with groundbreaking shifts on at least four important fronts: legislation and regulation, workforce demographics, leadership and succession, and advances in technology. Individually, each of these fronts is producing head-spinning complexity within the profession. Collectively, these changes can seem overwhelming and nearly impossible to conquer.

There is hope, though, and it lies in education. *Our* education. Specifically, our ability to learn our way *ahead* of the pace of change—and then, as Sheahan urges, to take action accordingly.

Tom Hood, a fixture on *Accounting Today's* annual list of the most influential people in accounting and my boss at the Maryland Association of CPAs, puts it this way: *In an era of great change, the most important skill we will possess going forward is the ability to learn new skills.*

How are *you* staying ahead of the change curve these days?

Want to change? Keep dancing.

Stop me if this sounds familiar.

You know you have to change. Complexity is hitting you from every angle, affecting every corner of your business.

Every fiber of your being screams, "Do something!"

And you just . . . can't.

Recognizing that things are changing is one thing. Doing something about them is another.

Why is change so hard?

Geoffrey Moore, the best-selling author of *Escape Velocity: Free Your Company's Future from the Pull of the Past,* said it's all about inertia.

"Our resources are trapped in the pull of the past. They want to stay where they are," Moore told the crowd at the 2012 DigitalNow Conference in Orlando. "The challenge is moving them in times of great change."

Sounds a lot like Peter Sheahan's "gravity of success," doesn't it? Funny how great ideas repeat themselves.

Think about it. We *know* we need to be doing something about social media, and mobile, and the cloud, and communities, and on-demand learning, and a ton of other things. And yet we can't break free of old, reliable, outdated habits like e-mail, and attached files, and PCs, and landlines, and classrooms. We've always done those things; we can't stop now, can we?

We'd better.

Doing so means "crossing the chasm"—that gaping space that separates the early adopters on our teams from the status-quo crowd. Crossing that chasm takes persistence. As Moore added in his speech, "Keep applying resources to your change effort, and eventually you'll hit a tipping point that will bring the rest of your team on board."

Think of it this way: *Keep dancing and eventually others will dance with you.*

It all comes down to engagement. Is your team on board with the change effort? Getting team members to that point, according to Moore, isn't about shiny new gadgets or cool new strategies. Sometimes, it's about convincing them that your organization's mission might be in peril if you *don't* change.

Isn't that true for all of us?

Three things you must do to conquer complexity.

I hear you saying, "You keep telling me the world is changing. You've told me over and over and over. *Now* tell me what I should do about it."

OK. Ask, as they say, and you shall receive.

For that information, let's bring in Rita McGrath. The Columbia Business School professor believes too many organizations are trying to solve today's complex problems with outdated methods. In short, they're trying to predict their way out of an unpredictable situation.

"One of the dilemmas we all face is that we're trying to grapple with truly complex systems using tools and frameworks designed for more simple, more linear systems," she told the crowd at the 2012 DigitalNow Conference in Orlando.

So what do we need to do? According to McGrath, three things:

1. Forecast differently.
2. Take on intelligent risk.
3. Allocate your resources differently.

1. Forecast differently.

Spend less time on *lagging* indicators like yesterday's numbers and outcomes. Spend more time on *leading* indicators like data that offer clues about what the future holds.

"Leading indicators are the hardest to find," McGrath said in her speech. "The problem is that they are subjective; they're not facts yet. But they also give us some distant early warnings about things that might happen."

Here's an exercise to try. Imagine a future event—something that's either good or bad for your organization. Now imagine what would have to happen first in order for that event to take place. Ask, "Can I see any signs that will tell me if that possibility is in the works now?"

2. Take on intelligent risk.

McGrath channeled political scientist Aaron Wildavsky for this one. Most organizations today invest in prevention—that is, trying to keep bad things from happening to them. McGrath said we need to invest more resources in what Wildavsky calls "resilience," a trait that will help us "mount the appropriate response" when something goes wrong.

That point of view requires an eye toward innovation. Simply stated, it means don't be afraid to try new things. If they work, great. If they don't, respond accordingly and try again.

"Start making small bets on things that are not part of your core business," McGrath said. "Then ask yourself, who are your truth-tellers—the people who can look at the future and articulate cases where things are going to be much different than they are today?"

And if the people in power aren't truth-tellers, watch out. This could be a difficult exercise.

3. Allocate your resources differently.
Sure, we need to focus on our core businesses. But in this crazy environment, McGrath said it's critical we also devote time and energy to innovation—identifying opportunities, thinking of things we'll want to invest in, figuring out how to ramp them up and make them scalable.

That means we'll also have to spend time on what she calls *disengagement*—figuring out what we should *stop* doing so we'll have the time and resources to devote to innovation.

And here's the most important thing: Your superstars need to be innovators. As McGrath said, "Average organizations put their best people on *problems*. Exceptional organizations put their best people on *opportunities*."

No room for big ideas? Make room.

Recently, my family and I played tourists in Chicago. We made our number one stop the Museum of Science and Industry, home of the German submarine U-505.

What an eye-popping exhibit! At 252 feet long, nearly 31 feet high, and 880 metric tons, the U-505 sank eight ships before the U.S. Navy captured it in the south Atlantic on June 4, 1944. It's one of only four World War II-era German U-boats in existence today as a museum ship. Students of World War II history need to make a beeline for Chicago to check this thing out.

Truth be told, though, I was more fascinated by how they got the monster inside the museum's basement. It's not like moving a couch; you don't just wiggle the thing through the front door and down the stairs.

As we were leaving the exhibit, I stopped to watch a video that explained this feat.

The U-505 arrived at the museum in 1954, and it sat on display on the MSI's lawn for the next 51 years. The sub took a beating from the elements, vandals, and a steady stream of tourists, so museum officials eventually decided to bring the U-505 inside.

To do it, they actually altered the museum itself. They built a new underground wing by digging a hole, lowering the sub into it, then walling it up and building an exhibit around it.

Genius.

What's my point? Simply this: The big changes that are rocking our worlds often don't fit neatly in the confines of our rigid business processes.

Too often, we try to change the new stuff to fit our needs.

But *we're* the ones who need to change.

Social media, the cloud, generational issues, the entire notion of leading through collaboration (rather than control)—these things don't fit our traditional business models. But guess what? They're dictating how business gets done going forward. We can't shoehorn these tools into a business-as-usual environment. They simply don't fit.

Therefore, we need to knock down a few walls and find space for it *where space didn't previously exist.*

What we do doesn't need to change. We're still committed to serving our members, our clients, our customers, and our employees. *How* we do that, though, has to change radically.

So stop talking and start listening. Stop selling services and start solving problems. Give away your knowledge and focus on offering your clients an honest-to-God *experience.*

In short, be human. Be social. Be *nice.*

Pretty radical, huh?

CHAPTER 2
LEAD

What does it mean to lead today? What separates the world's best leaders from the rest of the pack? Here's a guess: They use the word "we" more than the word "me."

Leadership today isn't about barking orders and command decisions. It's about nimbleness, flexibility, and collaboration.

At CPA Success, we've written a lot about the changing face of leadership. Here's a taste.

Good leaders just won't shut up.

Anyone who thinks talk is cheap has never met Emmanuel Gobillot.

An author, consultant, and one of Europe's most sought-after leadership speakers, Gobillot examines leadership in the context of today's social movement. He has reached this thought-provoking conclusion: *The most important weapon in today's leadership arsenal just might be conversation.*

"We can't accomplish anything without conversation," Gobillot said in a DigitalNow Conference keynote at Walt Disney World in Orlando. "Narratives are one of the most important leadership tools we have."

According to Gobillot, many leaders are doomed to fail because they don't pause long enough to notice the monumental changes around them. They're working so hard on *now* that they can't see *tomorrow* speeding toward them.

That sounds like a nugget of wisdom dropped by futurist Andrew Zolli, who said, "Great leaders scan the horizon for weak signals from the coming disruptive forces."

Well, once those signals are detected, the conversations should begin.

"Engaged people will do whatever it takes to get the job done," Gobillot said. "Engagement comes from conversation about the task at hand.

Those conversations lead to dreams of what could be, which lead to talk of what must be done."

In a DigitalNow tweet, fellow conference attendee Robert Rich described that idea as "dream, design, destiny"—a formula for inspiring people to work toward goals.

According to Gobillot, we can begin to measure that inspiring "dream, design, destiny" by asking one question: *Has this conversation made my team members feel stronger and more capable?*

"Did you ever notice when you're here at Disney World, you can't help but smile?" he pointed out. "Make your people as excited as you are. If you do that, you've got a Disney on your hands."

And that ain't bad.

Our DNA doesn't want us to change. Time for some genetic engineering.

We've spent a lot of time over the years asking how to battle change and complexity.

Turns out we've had the answer all along. All we have to do is be ourselves.

In his terrific book *You Are Now Less Dumb*, David McRaney says humans are genetically hardwired "to be optimistic in the face of futility."

It keeps us from giving up when we encounter hardships. When the chips are down, McRaney says we are programmed to see the silver lining.

It's all thanks to "positive illusions"—unrealistically favorable opinions that people form about themselves in times of severe stress or upheaval.

"Traits such as ambition, resolve, and group morale pushed human beings to cross oceans and tame crops," McRaney writes. "When the wind crushed those ships to splinters against impartial rocks, and those crops withered under an unsympathetic sun, your ancestors' positive illusions kicked in, biasing the downtrodden to see things in such a way that led to persistence, no matter how futile it must have seemed at times."

The more desperate our situation, McRaney writes, the more likely we are to see ourselves as indestructible.

"There is plenty of evidence that the odds are not in your favor, enough to deter you from trying just about everything in life," McRaney writes. "Luckily for you, most of the time you have no idea what you are getting into. . . . It makes sense that primates like you would have evolved a fondness for delusions of grandeur. That's the sort of attitude that gets you out of caves and beds."

There are some negatives to positive illusions, though.

Here's my new theory: The reason so many of us are resistant to change is that our positive illusions tell us we don't need to change. We don't need social media because we're awesome without it. We don't need to move to the cloud because we've done just fine without it. We don't need to worry about new business models because our current models are profit machines.

The problem with those positive illusions is that they make us just a bit too confident. We overestimate our ability to conquer change.

"On average, positive illusions work, but left unchecked, they can lead to terrible decisions and policies," McRaney writes. ". . . Occasionally, the same emotional state can mutate into hubris. . . . Since you are programmed to become increasingly overconfident the less you understand about any given scenario, you can expect to find the most destructive overconfidence in places that are exceedingly complicated and unpredictable."

In this day and age, is it possible that positive illusions keep us from changing when change is needed most? That they breed overconfidence in the present and ignorance of the future?

Maybe what we need right now are equal parts blind optimism and outright terror—faith that we need to change, and fear that we'll perish if we don't.

That's closer to the truth, after all.

Best business advice ever: Be willing to change.

My wife and I are huge Dave Barry fans, so when we heard that the Pulitzer Prize–winning humorist was coming to St. Louis, we made sure we were there—second row, center aisle.

You don't expect to find a life lesson in one of Barry's gut-busting stories, but there it was anyway, tucked inside a single sentence. Recalling the class-clown days of his youth, Barry told us, "My high school guidance counselor pulled me aside one day and said, 'Son, you'll never make a living being a smart ass.'"

Almost 50 years later, the scoreboard reads: Smart ass 1, guidance counselor 0.

His point, of course, is this: We spend too much time listening to other people tell us what we should do, and not enough time exploring the things that we want to do. If we look at them in the right light, we'll find those things are often one and the same.

It all depends on how you define your terms. A guidance counselor looks at a student and sees a smart ass. The student simply wants to make people laugh. "Smart ass" isn't much of a career trajectory, but making people laugh? There are a million ways to do that.

In the same light, many people hear "accountant" and think they know exactly what you do, and why? Because it's always been done that way. Truth is, the traditional definitions of "accountant" don't fit anymore. We're quickly moving toward an era where accountants spend less time looking at the past and more time helping clients prepare for the future. People might call you an accountant, but what you're really doing is solving problems.

Advances in technology have a lot to do with that, but the IT world is dealing with the same issue.

"Right now, we take new technology and give it to an architect who sees the world as it was yesterday," best-selling author Brian Solis writes. ". . . They see something new and put it into a familiar box, just because this is the way it's always been done. They take something that's native to a new world and force it to comply within a legacy paradigm defined by dated philosophies, systems, and reward systems."

New stuff doesn't fit neatly into the rigid confines of our closed minds. The latest technology won't work for us because we don't work that way. You won't succeed because you don't think like us. We don't need to change because we're already making plenty of money.

Most of us are still living in a world of round pegs and round holes. When a square peg shows up, what's the first thing we do? Look for a round peg to take its place. We don't stop to consider that we might need to drill a few square holes instead. We try to force new things to work the way the way we do, then get frustrated when they won't.

Maybe we're the ones who need to change.

"The only way to take a meaningful step forward," Solis writes, "is to understand how to adapt legacy investments, systems and processes to pave the way for a more engaging and productive future for all."

So let's make room for a few smart asses. They're going to find a way to succeed anyway.

It might as well be with you.

Three questions for tomorrow's leaders: Don't flunk this quiz.

The CPA profession needs new leaders. We need 'em by the truckload.

Here's the problem: We're training tomorrow's leaders to work like yesterday's leaders.

So says Roselinde Torres, a leadership expert and managing director at the New York office of The Boston Consulting Group.

In a recent TED talk, Torres said more than half of today's businesses aren't prepared to turn the reins over to new leadership. Why? Because the ways in which they've trained their new leaders are woefully outdated, "based largely on success models for a world that was, not a world that is or that is coming," she said.

"In a world that is more global, digitally enabled and transparent, with faster speeds of information flow and innovation, and where nothing big gets done without some kind of a complex matrix, relying on traditional development practices will stunt your growth as a leader," Torres said.

So how do we define 21st-century leadership? Torres said we'll find the answer by asking ourselves three questions:

- Where are you looking for life's next big changes? Torres says you can answer that question with a series other questions: Who are you spending time with? On what topics? Where are you traveling? What are you reading? How are you distilling all of this information into decisions about tomorrow? "Great leaders are not heads-down," Torres said. "They see around corners, shaping their future, not just reacting to it."

- How diverse is your network? The more it crosses biological, physical, functional, political, cultural, or socioeconomic boundaries, the better. "Great leaders understand that having a more diverse network is a source of solutions, because you have people who are thinking differently than you."

- Are you courageous enough to abandon a practice that has made you successful in the past? "Great leaders dare to be different," Torres said. "They don't just talk about risk-taking, they actually do it. . . . Interestingly, the people who will join you are not the usual suspects in your network. They're often people who think differently and therefore are willing to join you in taking a courageous leap—and it's a leap, not a step."

Interesting, isn't it, how all of these things come down to you. Where are you looking for change? Who are you adding to your network? What risks are you taking?

It's all about choices, people.

Actually, it's all about a single choice: Will you choose to lead in a changing and complex world?

If the answer is "yes," the rest will fall into place.

A 6-step guide to changing the world.

We all have grand plans to change the world.

And then life gets in the way.

That's reality, isn't it? Despite all of the need for change, innovation, and outright intervention, most of us are too busy living our own lives to make a difference.

So how does that difference get made?

How does someone like Adam Braun found one of the world's most innovative philanthropic organizations, one that's dedicated to educating children in areas of the world where education doesn't exist? How does he build more than 200 schools from the ground up in less than four years, then end up on *Wired* magazine's list of "50 People Changing the World?" How does he earn a Distinguished American Leadership Award, and a Fast Company Innovation Agent award, and a spot on *Forbes'* "30 Under 30 list" in the same year?

Through foresight, and service, and a whole lot of courage.

Braun, founder and executive director of Pencils of Promise, stopped by the DigitalNow Conference in Nashville to share his story. And while it's clear that few of us have the time or the will to do the kinds of world-changing things that Braun has done, we can each make a difference in our own way. Braun offered some words of wisdom to help us take the first step.

Find your passion
Live with your eyes open. Be open to the idea that your most important work lies ahead. A near-death

experience aboard a ship during the Semester at Sea program forced Braun to re-evaluate his purpose in life, as did a chance encounter with a young boy in India during the same trip. Braun asked the boy what he would want if he could have anything in the world. The boy answered, "A pencil." Connecting pencils to education, Braun found his way. "There is nothing more powerful than discovering your purpose," he said. "You become unstoppable."

Tell the world

That's not true, though. You become unstoppable only when you act on that purpose, and that's more difficult than it sounds. As our busy lives roll on, it's easy to make excuses for why we can't do something new. Breaking the gravity of the status quo might be as simple as telling the world what you want to do. Want to quit smoking, or lose 10 pounds, or start a new business that might just change the world? Tell everyone you know. It'll drive you to action, and you might find a few partners at the same time. "Say what you want to do out loud," Braun said. "Speak the language of the person you want to become."

Serve others

As we chase our own dreams, too often we forget why we do what we do. Case in point: Non-profit organizations. "I hate that term," Braun said. "We're not non-profits. We're for-purpose." True happiness, he said, is found in service to others. "Every single one of us has the ability to change a life for the better," Braun added. "We just have to believe it." And be committed to it, he didn't have to add.

Take risks

What got us here won't get us there. In a world as chaotic as this, said Braun, "(the) only way to lead in our space is to keep innovating."

Get uncomfortable

Eleanor Roosevelt's belief that we should do one thing every day that scares us is more than an overused business cliche. There is true power in escaping our comfort zones. How can we possibly hope to make a difference if we don't try new things? Braun drove that point home by channeling Liberian President Ellen Johnson Sirleaf: "If your dreams do not scare you," he said, "they are not big enough."

Embrace your inner underdog

"I get inspired by people who take on challenges that others deem impossible," Braun told me after his presentation. "I get inspired by the underdog. That's why I love March Madness—I want the 15 (seed) to make it to the Final Four. As a culture, I think we're inspired by stories of people who overcome adversity. It demonstrates that the improbable things can be made real, and that it takes real courage to try."

You can hear more about Braun's story at http://cpa.tc/4xn.

Is it the end of (your) business?

> "In an era of Digital Darwinism, no business is too big to fail or too small to succeed."
> — Brian Solis

Blockbuster, Circuit City, Borders, Pontiac, CompUSA—where are they today?

In his book *The End of Business as Usual: Rewire the Way You Work to Succeed in the Consumer Revolution,* Brian Solis, best-selling author and principal at Altimeter Group, a research firm focused on disruptive technology, argued that these companies fell victim to the forces of natural selection, what he called "digital Darwinism."

I found Brian's message compelling because it reinforces patterns and trends I see emerging through the fog of the recession—that maybe this recession is not only about the fallout of the housing bubble or the actions of Bernie Madoff.

Maybe it's not only about Wall Street greed.

Maybe we are going through an inflection point, a period of dramatic change that can alter the path our organization travels.

Business guru Professor Gary Hamel is quoted as saying, "Accepting social power as inevitable . . . the underlying principles on the web of natural hierarchy, transparency, collaboration and all the rest are going to have to invade management." ("Social Power and the Coming Corporate Revolution: Why Employees and Customers Will Be Calling the Shots," *Forbes*, September 2011, http://cpa.tc/2ec)

Fast Company editor Robert Safian opened the February 2012 "Generation Flux" issue of his magazine this way: "In our hyper-networked, mobile, social, global world, the rules and plans of yesterday are increasingly under pressure; the enterprises and individuals that will thrive will be those willing to adapt and iterate, in a disciplined, unsentimental way ("This Is Generation Flux: Meet the Pioneers of the New (And Chaotic) Frontier of Business," *Fast Company*, January 2012, http://cpa.tc/2ed)

We face a tsunami of forces that are rapidly changing the business environment. Globalization, demographics, and technology are combining and magnifying the size, scale, and scope of business challenges today.

This describes an inflection point that Andy Grove, former CEO of Intel Corporation, used to talk about in the 1990s this way:

"It's the point in the life of a business or industry when its fundamentals are about to change. The change can mean an opportunity to rise to new heights. But it may just as likely signal the beginning of the end. They build up force so insidiously that you may have a hard time putting your finger on what has changed, but you know something has. It's that time when something is changing in a big way, when something is different . . . that the signals

of change only become clear in retrospect."
("The Education of Andy Grove," *Fortune*,
December 2005, http://cpa.tc/2ee)

Still not convinced? Watch Brian Solis's video
message at http://www.youtube.com/watch?v=W-
Yf1u3xD_I. The closing lines in his video sum-
marize it all:

> "Many follow, but very few lead. Many
> compete to survive, but few compete for
> **relevance.** Do we listen to our customers?
> Do we truly understand them? Do we
> create experiences, or do we simply react?

> "The future of business comes down to
> one word: **Change.**

> "This is a new era that redefines every-
> thing, an **era of empowered consum-
> ers and employees.** Will we fall to natu-
> ral selection or will we rise to lead the
> revolution?

> "This is our time to make business relevant,
> because people, after all, are **everything.**"

Think of Brian's book as a field guide to this new chaotic world, an antidote to natural selection.

Is it the end of business as we know it? What will you do to escape the forces of "digital Darwinism?"

This post by Tom Hood, CEO of MACPA.

The secret to leadership success? Try the periwinkles.

My wife Alison has a non-negotiable rule about eating out: Don't order anything you'd make for yourself at home. No chicken. No salmon. No spaghetti. If you're going to lay out that kind of cash for a meal, make it an experience.

She took that rule to an extreme for my 2012 birthday dinner. We went to an incredible place called Stone Soup Cottage, just west of St. Louis. This place opened in 2009; by 2010, it had been named the top restaurant in St. Louis. It's *that* good.

When you go to Stone Soup Cottage, you eat what *they* decide to feed you. There's no menu with a million options. In fact, you're given a list of what you'll be eating that night—take it or leave it. It's called a tasting menu with six small courses, some of them paired with wine.

Right away, I liked it. No menu meant no decisions and fewer things to worry about. I didn't even mind that two of the courses featured truffles (which I hate) and that a third consisted entirely of something called "periwinkles" (obviously a fictional food). No matter—this was going to be a God's honest *experience*.

And it was. Simply put, it might have been the best meal I've ever had. Because the chef wasn't spread too thin with an overpopulated menu, he could concentrate on thoughtfully and artfully preparing a few things. Heaven!

So what's the point?

Here it is, leaders: *Take a few chances every now and then.*

Sure, you can choose the safe route, do the same old tired thing over and over again, and produce the same old results. You might even make money doing it.

Here's what you *won't* do:

- Stay relevant.
- Improve yourself.
- Learn anything new.

- Stay on top of the latest trends.
- Help your *clients* stay on top of the latest trends.
- Notice the weak signals of disruptive change and the game-changing opportunities they provide.

Remember the formula stated at the beginning—that your learning must be greater than the rate of change. Yes, it's possible to keep coasting ignorantly along until change crushes you.

But do yourself a favor: Try the periwinkles.

I learned all I need to know from fourth grade basketball.

My daughter Molly played fourth grade basketball this year. In her first foray into team sports, she learned really important stuff—the one-hand dribble, the virtues of boxing out, the bizarre randomness of the three-second rule, and more. Previously, this girl wouldn't watch anything on TV that didn't involve teen rock stars. And I actually caught her paying attention to a Mizzou (Missouri State) basketball game the other day.

Here's the deal, though, and I mean this: *Important life and leadership lessons are being taught to fourth grade basketball players.* Consider these:

- **This game's not about you.** Many other folks have a stake in this thing, too. Work together and you can perform miracles. Work alone and you're doomed.

- **Learn the fundamentals.** Dunks and no-look assists might land you on SportsCenter, but you won't get there unless you learn how to dribble, pass, and shoot first—the basics.

- **Improvise.** We all have set plays we like to run. Our opponents want to stop us. Sometimes we have to ditch the game plan and try something else. Don't be afraid to do that. Life is all about rolling with the punches.

- **Be aggressive.** You won't get what you want by sitting around watching someone else drive to the hoop. Go after the ball. Give and go. Set the tempo, or it will get set for you. Do you want to determine your own future, or let others determine it for you?

- **Cheer on your teammates.** A little encouragement goes a long way. This is a team, after all. When one of us wins, we all win, right?

- **Be a good winner *and* a good loser.** Saying a few "nice games" and "way-to-go's" will take you a long way. You'll be on the other side of every outcome eventually. How you react in each situation will define you in the long run.

Finally—and I can't stress this enough—plant that pivot foot. Even if you *are* in fourth grade, you *will* be called for traveling.

Leaders don't guess. They turn insights into action.

I vote that we ban all economic forecasts and surveys from now until the end of time. Ban 'em like asbestos.

Why? Read these September 2011 titles of economic forecasts and weep. Or laugh.

- "CFO Optimism Plummets" (from CFO.com)
- "CFOs Feel Cautiously Optimistic" (from *Accounting Today*)

- "A Double Dip? CFOs Are Divided" (from CFO.com)
- "Little Hiring Growth Planned for 2012" (from *Harvard Business Review*)
- "CPAs' Economic Outlook Drops in Third Quarter" (from the AICPA)
- "Survey Shows Hiring Plans Rising for Accountants, Other Professionals" (from the *Journal of Accountancy*)

Got that? The economy stinks. But not really. And we're hiring! Maybe. And optimism abounds! Except for those pessimists over there. And blah, blah, blah.

Here's a prediction you can take to the bank: *Guessing isn't going to solve any of our problems.*

Neither is blaming the other guy, by the way.

Want to know how many jobs have been created by political one-upmanship? None. Zero. Zip.

That's why we need politicians who are willing to work across party lines to solve the big problems of the day. Instead, we're getting pure political hatred, and that accomplishes nothing.

Where are our leaders?

Sitting in on the Maryland Association of CPAs' three-day Leadership Academy, I was blown away by what I saw. A room full of 40 of the profession's best and brightest—young CPAs who want to make a difference—worked *together* to draft a vision for the profession going forward. In three days, 40 people from incredibly diverse backgrounds agreed unanimously on six bold initiatives that could reshape the profession.

Three days, one bold vision.

You're telling me Congress can't do the same? I'm telling you they *need* to.

Let's stop guessing and hating, people. Let's start working together.

Top five skills of the post-recession leader.

Could this be the decade of the CPA?

It started in 2010, which *The Economist* proclaimed as the Year of the CFO. Now, *Chief Learning Officer* says the best CEO will be part CFO and part COO, which means the core financial and analytical skills of the CPA are more important than ever.

An article in *Chief Learning Officer* titled "The Post-Recession Leader: Part CEO, COO and CFO" examines the most valuable leadership skills in this post-recession world. Here's my take on five of the most important skills today's leaders must have:

1. Broader and longer line of sight—the ability to see emerging patterns and shift perspective when necessary.

2. Network leadership—the ability to connect various stakeholders, including customers, regulators, team members, investors, and supply chain partners.

3. Strong analytical skills (financial and operational)—a strong and working understanding of the business and operations at an economic and financial level. (CPAs, you already have this!)

4. Communication skills—the ability to communicate effectively and simplify complex issues in a way that people will easily "get."

5. Global perspective—the world is flat, and all leaders today need to develop a global perspective and some international skills.

In the *Chief Learning Officer* article, Stephen Miles, vice chairman of the executive recruitment firm Heidrick & Struggles, said, "The best CEOs in the world are a combination of CEO, COO, and CFO. They are inspirational, financially literate, and know the ins and outs of their business at a sophisticated level."

Now we're talking. The skill sets of the CPA are back in vogue. Companies need smart spending and careful evaluation of their investments using *real numbers*. Thus the CPA brings disciplined thinking, financial literacy, and an understanding of the business that few can match.

Even if you don't aspire to the corner office, this is an opportunity to make a difference for your organizations and clients. *They need CPAs more than ever.* And if you do aspire to move up that career ladder, acquire more of those right-brain skills and become an "ambidextrous" thinker.

The leader of the future must be able to think both critically and creatively.

This lines up with our own research from the Business Learning Institute on the top five qualities of extraordinary leaders:

1. Sight—the ability to see emerging patterns and shift perspective when necessary.

2. Insight—the ability to learn faster than the rate of change in your industry.

3. Creativity—the ability to think strategically and critically to gain insights that create new opportunities.

4. Communication Skills—the ability to collaborate inside and outside your organization and to build and sustain social networks.

5. Inspiration Skills—the ability to mobilize support and engage others to join you in action.

Leadership isn't about "command and control" any longer. Today, it's about "communication and collaboration"—with a healthy dose of continuous learning thrown into the mix.

The new boss of today is decidedly *not* the same as the old boss of yesterday.

This post by Tom Hood, CEO of MACPA.

CHAPTER 3
LOVE

The word "Love" covers a lot of ground. Love of family. Love of life. Love of work, justice, and your fellow man. It's the notion that there's something greater than self-interest at work here. We're here to serve, not be served. Once we learn that, the world is ours.

Life sometimes has funny ways of teaching us lessons in love. Here are several of our favorites.

Want people to be nice? Be nice first.

It was raining in New York. LaGuardia Airport was mobbed, and one look at the "big board" told the story: Nearly every departing flight was delayed, and not just by a few minutes. We're talking two-, maybe three-hour delays, the kind that make people really, really grumpy.

Except almost no one was grumpy.

They were sharing tables and chairs at the terminal's lone, overcrowded bar. Air-travel veterans were plugging in multi-outlet chargers and making new friends of the strangers who stopped by to charge their iPhones. In line to board their flights, folks were joking about how there would be more room on the plane than in the crowded terminal. Flight attendants smiled and laughed as they welcomed people aboard.

By all rights, it should have been a miserable wait. Instead, it was almost . . . fun.

Turns out humanity still has a surprise or two up its sleeve.

But you know what? We can kickstart those surprises by smiling first, by offering the seat or telling the joke or being the charging-station hero.

Interesting concept, huh? Maybe we're the ones who are responsible for making life pleasant.

It's not what you take that counts—it's what you give.

Inspiration is everywhere. You just have to open your eyes.

During the Annual Convention of the National Association of Black Accountants, I had the privilege of having lunch with Daniel Worrell, director of internal controls for the Metropolitan Transportation Authority in New York City, who said the most amazing thing about halfway through the meal.

To paraphrase Daniel's thoughts:

We go to conferences, and CPE programs, and networking events intent on learning as much as we can—of grabbing as much value as we can get our hands on and taking it home. And with good reason—the only way to conquer change is to out-learn it, right?

Here's Daniel's question, though:

How many of us go to these events intent on leaving something behind?

It's true: The most important skill we'll need going forward is the ability to learn new skills. "Serial mastery," London Business School professor Lynda Gratton calls it.

Equally important, though—maybe more important—is our ability to add value to other people's lives. To share what we know with our followers. To help our clients solve problems. To build relationships through generosity.

Do that often enough and you'll build your business at the same time.

The next time you go to a conference, or a CPE program, or a networking event, think not only about the value you want to get, but of the value you want to give. What are you going to leave behind? What great questions are you going to ask? What thought-provoking insights are you going to offer? What problems are you going to solve? What relationships are you going to build?

To paraphrase JFK, *think not of what others can do for you, but of what you can do for others.*

That's the sweet spot of social business—where we give in order to receive.

Thinking of others first is the essence of the social movement—and really, it's just the right thing to do.

Can't do it? Tell me what you can do.

I don't want to hear your excuses.

Don't tell me your life is difficult. Don't tell me you're too busy to innovate, or learn something new, or become future-ready. Don't you dare tell me that doing all of this new stuff is too hard.

You don't know what hard is.

If you're willing to listen, though, Brad Snyder will tell you.

Snyder is a Navy veteran and a member of the Navy's elite bomb disposal squad. He was permanently blinded in 2011 when an improvised explosive device (or IED) exploded while he was working on it in Afghanistan.

He went to Afghanistan to serve his country, and he came back blind. Want to know what he's done since then?

- He won a gold medal in the 100-meter free-style swimming competition at the 2012 Paralympics in London.

- He became a leading veterans' advocate through his work with the COMMIT Foundation, which helps veterans transition successfully back into civilian life.

- He has become an inspirational speaker who offers advice on overcoming adversity to anyone who will listen.

Snyder told that story as part of the Maryland Association of CPAs' Innovation Summit in Baltimore.

His most important message? This is about what you *can* do, not what you can't.

"From early on," Snyder said, "my family and I strategically put an emphasis on these questions: 'What does the way forward look like? How do I do all the things I used to do, and how do I make things as normal as possible?' If you put all of your eggs in that basket, you forget about the fact that you can't see and you remember that you can still hear, and run, and swim. You fill up the time with the things you can do, and you don't really have time left to think about the things you can't do. I've done that long enough now that I don't even feel blind. I feel that this is just the way life is now."

Put another way: We're so uptight about the negatives that we completely miss the positives.

- Maybe we don't have time to master every social network . . . but we might have time to master one of them.

- Maybe we're too busy to regroup and do truly innovative, groundbreaking work . . . but we might be able to pause long enough to ask a few future-focused questions that will lead to meaningful change for our organizations.

· Maybe we're overloaded with information . . . but we might be able to learn how to use a couple of powerful tools that will filter that information and let us focus on just the valuable stuff.

"It's all about perspective," Snyder said. "Every situation, every person, every entity, every set of circumstances you find yourself in—if you look for the good in those circumstances, you'll find it. You have to make that deliberate choice: I am going to find the good in people and my own circumstances. If you make a habit of doing that, you will empower yourself to be successful."

Do that long enough and you'll forget that you're blind—especially if you're wearing a gold medal around your neck.

Connections work. Need proof? Ask 'the name tag guy.'

Fourteen years ago and fresh out of college, Scott Ginsberg made a truly bizarre decision.

He was going to wear a name tag everywhere he went. All the time. Twenty-four hours a day, seven days a week.

And why?

"When you wear a name tag, people are instantly friendlier," he told the crowd at a TEDx Gateway Arch event in St. Louis.

It was a lark, really. But then he moved to Oregon and told some guy on a bus about his name tag. That guy told his girlfriend, who happened to be a reporter for the Portland newspaper. She called Scott and asked if she could write an article about his name tag.

Then *USA Today* called. Then the morning TV talk shows called. Then he wrote a book. Then organizations started asking him to speak at their events.

Then he wrote 26 more books.

Today, his unofficial title is "Name Tag Guy." That's what he does for a living. He wears a name tag and talks about it. He even had a name tag tattooed on his chest, so that he could wear one every second of every day.

And it all started with a conversation with a complete stranger on a bus.

"How many strangers did you avoid today?" Ginsberg asked the TEDx crowd in St. Louis. "Everyone you meet is somebody's somebody."

In other words: Connections work. Networks work. Relationships work.

And one more thing:

"If you don't make a name for yourself," he said, "someone else will make it for you."

We're at a crossroads here, CPAs. Sure, times are complex. Sure, doing business is harder than ever. But we have access to tools that will make it easier—tools that will help us make connections, build networks, and grow.

Tools that will help us find somebody's somebody.

When we do that, making a name for ourselves becomes ridiculously easy.

Which leads us to Ginsberg's final lesson:

"The question isn't, 'Should I wear a name tag?'" he said. "The question is, 'What's my name tag?'"

What's yours?

Social business starts with how you treat your team.

This social business fad? It's no fad.

You know an idea has legs when you start seeing it everywhere, and my friends, social business is everywhere.

I found myself with some down time on a recent business trip, so I re-read Jeanne Bliss's terrific book *I Love You More Than My Dog*, in which she examines what differentiates "beloved companies"—the ones with devoted, fanatical customers—from the competition. The following passage blew my mind:

"What sets companies that customers love apart from the others is that they imagine the (customer) experience first. Then—and only then—can they deliver it."

In other words, amazing things happen when you start thinking like your customers—when your focus switches from selling something to solving problems.

That point was driven home at the American Institute of CPAs' annual Digital CPA Conference. CPAs love to describe themselves as "trusted business advisors," but as Succession Institute co-founder and CEO Bill Reeb warned the crowd, "You can't be a trusted advisor unless you know what's keeping your clients up at night."

Think like your clients. Solve their problems, not your own. Be human. The message couldn't be clearer.

Then Simon Sinek took the stage.

You remember Simon. He's the guy who wrote the remarkable *Start With Why* and recorded the second most-watched TED talk to date—and if you haven't watched it yet, you simply must. You can find it at http://cpa.tc/4xo.

At Digital CPA, he took a new path—one based on his forthcoming book *Leaders Eat Last* and related to the think-like-a-client movement, but with a twist:

"Your clients and customers will never love you," he said, "unless your employees love you first."

How do you do that? By making them feel safe.

Building a "circle of safety" that surrounds your entire team will empower them to take chances, make them feel trusted, and foster greater collaboration across your organization. That will make them feel stronger and more capable and inspire them to act on your clients' behalf.

"How do we inspire and drive change?" Sinek asked. "Look out for the people to the left and right of you."

In other words, take care of your team, and they'll take care of your clients.

Pretty simple concept. The lesson is pretty clear: Think of your people first.

Do that, and your profits will take care of themselves.

Sure, you might get hurt—but go play anyway.

My wife Alison and I spent the evening at the local urgent care center watching a doctor attend to our nine-year-old daughter's bruised and oddly misshapen right wrist.

Talk about a buzz-kill.

It was March 12, 2012. Still technically winter, for God's sake, but the thermometer read about 80 degrees under sunny skies. Once the homework's done, what's a kid to do except sprint out the back door and head straight to the nearest jungle gym?

There are risks, of course. Our daughter learned that the hard way. The cast she wore for the next eight weeks was an uncomfortable reminder.

But what was she supposed to do—sit inside and watch TV? On a day like *that*?

And because the really cool stuff comes with risks, we've got two choices:

- We can chicken out, take no chances, and keep plodding along in uninspiring mediocrity, or

- We can run outside and try something new, something fun, something that will keep us healthy and expand our horizons—something that will lead to great things.

Once Molly's cast came off, what did she do? Headed straight out the back door.

All things being equal, like my daughter, I'd rather deal with an occasional broken wrist than miss out on the chance to play again on the jungle gym.

Stuff happens. How will you respond?

There I was at Lambert International Airport in St. Louis. Not a cloud in the sky. My plane sat at the gate with passengers ready to board—all systems go.

Only trouble was, nasty storms were sitting on top of Baltimore, my destination. In short, we weren't going anywhere. A ground stop. The first 30 minutes passed. Then 60. Then 90. Two hours past our departure time and we weren't even close to boarding our plane.

There's a life lesson in there somewhere, and I think it's this: *Stuff happens.* Nothing you can do. The question is, how are you going to respond when it does?

At Lambert, we had two options: We could get angry, frustrated, out of sorts, and, as my wife likes to say, experience "a little piece of misery." Or we could take a deep breath, realize everyone else was in the same boat, and put the time to good use. I saw examples of both that day.

Time magazine recently published an article that examined the ways people respond to life-threatening emergencies ("A Survival Guide to Catastrophe," *Time*, May 2008). Overwhelmingly, it indicated the people who survive emergencies are those who keep their heads and take charge of the situation.

"Survival is not just a product of luck," wrote the article's author, Amanda Ripley. "We can do far more than we think to improve our odds of preventing and surviving even the most horrendous of catastrophes. It's a matter of preparation . . .

but also of mental conditioning. Each of us has what I call a 'disaster personality,' a state of being that takes over in a crisis. It is at the core of who we are. The fact is, we can refine that personality and teach our brains to work more quickly, maybe even more wisely."

This author might be onto something. I think our "disaster personalities" can be applied to minor setbacks as well, and they can go a long way toward determining our state of mind when life's annoyances pop up—like they did that day at Lambert Airport.

How do you react when things go awry? What do you do to turn the situation to your advantage?

Passion or bust.

Have you ever had one of those moments when someone says something so profound, so right-eously perfect, that it makes you take stock of everything you believe?

I have. It happened during the 2011 AICPA E.D.G.E. Conference in New Orleans, a leadership skills event for young CPA professionals.

During a panel discussion titled "Sky High: Personal Success Stories," Nicole Morris explained why she turned her back on the corporate fast track to teach the next generation of CPAs as an accounting professor at Champlain College.

"I decided not to do anything I'm not passionate about," she told the crowd. After this radical idea set my head spinning, I stopped and thought: What if we *all* did that? How different would the world be? How much happier? How much more productive? How completely *awesome*?

We only get one shot at this thing called life, folks. It's simply too short to do things that suck. So find your passion. Get good at it. Work hard. Demand excellence from yourself.

And guess what? That passion is contagious. Others will follow your lead.

A pipe dream? Maybe. Too many people settle for *good enough* these days. And what a cop-out that is. Good enough isn't nearly enough—not at work, not at home, not in anything you do. Not when you put it in the context of one singular life.

Success isn't rocket science: Be nice. That will do.

Nice guys finish last? Not in Tim Sanders's world.

He's not alone, of course. The antiquated notion that says you have to be a bastard to get to the top has been rotting in the corporate landfill for a while now.

Sanders, though, goes even further. Not only is it OK to be nice—it is absolutely essential.

The best-selling author of *Love Is the Killer App*, *the Likeability Factor*, and *Today We Are Rich* (which is required reading, in my opinion) offers this straightforward message:

Relationships matter.

Check that. Relationships don't simply matter; they might be the *only* things that matter.

"Your network defines your net worth," Sanders said during his keynote at the 2011 CCH User Conference in San Antonio. "Relationship quality is *everything*." So if relationships are the only things that matter, what must we do to take advantage of that fact?

Sanders offers these ideas:

Don't hire unhappy people: Your culture is at stake the minute you sit down to interview a potential employee. Too often, we focus on a prospect's skill sets. But the most important factor is not performance; it's happiness.

High-performance jerks suck the life out of the office. Hire for happiness first and performance second.

This is vitally important. If you hire happy people, your office will be a happy place to work. How much more pleasant, productive, and progressive will you be if your employees are happy and engaged? I don't need to provide the answer.

Smile. A smile says, "I like you. I appreciate you." That creates a culture of friendliness, making life at the office infinitely better.

If friendliness is top priority, relevance is a not-too-distant second. Relevance is the only thing that keeps relationships going. And since relationships matter, *relevance* matters. You add value to your clients' lives by being relevant.

Be generous. Mentor others. Give away the stuff you know. Network relentlessly. And keep this in mind: Networking is *not* about you. It's about connecting people to other people and then getting out of the way. If you do that well, it will come back to you.

Be empathetic. *Feel* for the other person. Feelings are facts. "You shouldn't feel that way" is not an appropriate response. To reach the pinnacle of relationship success, be emotionally available. Treat all feelings as facts. Listen. Respond. If you do that, you'll have become the most important person in your clients' lives.

My mother's favorite saying comes from the Disney movie *Bambi*:

> *"If you can't say anything nice,*
> *don't say anything at all."*

Based on what Tim Sanders tells us, I might change that to say:

> *"If you can't say anything nice,*
> *you're doomed to fail."*

That's because in today's social world, relationships *do* matter. Friendliness is essential. Relevance is non-negotiable. Add value and do it nicely. Fail to do that, and you risk becoming irrelevant.

It's your choice.

Does your customer service drive clients wild?

What are your expectations when you take a cab?

If you're like me, they're pretty low: A quick "Where ya going?" and a high-speed run to the hotel about covers it. I'm usually happy if I make actual eye contact with the driver; a smile is a bonus. Help me with my bags and you'll get the biggest tip you've gotten all day.

So imagine my surprise when I landed in Fort Myers, Florida, and took the most enjoyable cab ride of my life.

The woman at the cab stand smiled and greeted me with a friendly "How are you?" She asked me where I was going, told me the fee up front, explained that, yes, the driver takes American Express, and sent me off with—believe it or not— another smile and a "Thank you."

And that was all before I climbed into the cab.

The driver was all smiles; she lifted my bags into the trunk, held the door, and chatted with me as we made our way to the hotel. When I had to make a call, she fell respectfully silent. On occasion, she pointed out area landmarks, explained what "Fiddlesticks" is (a local country club), and graciously turned a normally forgettable 25-minute cab ride into a pleasant experience.

I know what you're saying. "Don't get too worked up, Bill. It was just a cab ride."

You know what, though? It was more than that.

It was a textbook example of going above and beyond on behalf of a client, of working your tail off to find that extra degree, of distinguishing yourself from the competition by doing the most basic thing possible—pleasing your customer. Don't sell them services; solve their problems. Don't talk; listen. Remember who you work for, and here's a hint: It's not your employer.

So here's to the folks at MBA Airport Transportation. They get it. And if you're ever flying through Fort Myers, look 'em up. I'd be willing to bet they'll make it worth your while.

Social media's promise: Be nice, or pay a price.

Here at CPA Success, we've spent a lot of time talking about the ways in which the social media movement has transformed our world. Our networks are bigger than ever. We have more opportunities to learn than we've ever had. We can serve our customers and expand our personal brands in ways we've never experienced before.

And still people like to talk about social media's alleged problems: loss of control, privacy issues, return on investment, time management, and more.

You know what the real problem is, though? In a social world, you can't fake it.

Humorist Dave Barry puts it this way: "A person who is nice to you but rude to the waiter is not a nice person."

Put another way: If you're combative by nature, your true colors will shine through sooner or later.

Thanks to social media, we're learning that lesson over and over.

- Remember United Breaks Guitars? An airline broke a musician's guitar, then refused to take responsibility for its actions. One song, one YouTube video, and 13 million views later, the airline learned its lesson and worked to make amends.

- Remember *Cooks Source*? A small, New England magazine published a blogger's article without permission or payment, then responded rudely to the blogger's e-mail request for compensation and an apology. When the magazine's response went viral, the online world flew into a rage. The publisher's assertion that all web content is considered to be in the public domain was widely and rudely criticized by tens of thousands of online commenters. The magazine shut down its operations shortly after.

· Remember Paul Christoforo? He was a PR contact and customer service rep for a manufacturer of game controllers. In response to an impatient customer's inquiry about the status of an order, Christoforo responded, in part, by telling the customer to "put on your big boy hat and wait it out like everyone else." The magnitude of that mistake was seemingly surpassed only by Christoforo's ego. Anyone who believes the crowd should cut him some slack because "ultimately I'm not a bad guy" doesn't understand the world we're living in.

You're not a bad guy? Prove it by treating your customers—all of your customers—with dignity and respect.

The lesson here is simple. Be nice. All the time. To everyone.

We'll almost never get in trouble if we do that. In fact, we'll win more fans than we ever dreamed of.

The famed Leo Durocher was wrong. In a social media world, nice guys finish *first*.

Customer service champs? If the shoe fits . . .

Maybe good customer service isn't an endangered species after all.

Sure, there are plenty of horror stories out there, but many pretty good ones, too.

And because I'm a sucker for this touchy-feely stuff, I've got yet another one for you.

We buy all of our daughter's shoes at a place called Laurie's. It's kind of a St. Louis institution. My wife has been wearing Laurie's shoes since she first started walking, so *of course* that's where we buy our daughter's footwear. And they've got the kid stuff down pat, too—balloons, cookies, TV, a *slide*, for Pete's sake.

It's as close to paradise as a kid's shoe-shopping trip can get.

Laurie's also sells shoes for adults. So my wife found herself there recently, in search of a nice pair of walking shoes. "They're for our trip to Orlando," Alison told Kristi, the salesperson. "We're taking our daughter to Disney World for spring break."

A couple of days later, our daughter Molly received a hand-written note from Kristi in the mail. It read simply, "Have a fabulous trip! We'll look forward to seeing you when you get back!"

Sappy? Sure. Corny? You bet. Ulterior motives? Lots of 'em.

Effective? Like you wouldn't believe.

We were sold on Laurie's before. But now? They've got us spreading the word. And why? Because Kristi *listened*. For a couple of moments, my wife's story was the most important thing on Kristi's mind. As a result, when it comes to shoes, Laurie's is the most important thing on *our* minds.

That's good customer service in a nutshell. Your customer is happy, and *you* benefit as a result. It's not rocket science.

It kind of reminds me of a conference I attended a couple of years ago. The event was held at a Ritz-Carlton, and a colleague told the following story:

Months before the conference, this colleague called the Ritz to reserve her room. After the transaction was complete, the lady who took the reservation asked, "Is there anything else I can do for you?"

"Well, you could have Brad Pitt waiting for me in my room when I arrive," she joked, and everyone had a good laugh.

Fast-forward to the conference check-in. When my colleague entered her room at the Ritz, lying on her bed was a framed photo of Brad Pitt.

It's not so much the gesture. It's the fact that people bothered to *listen*. And it works.

If you can't say anything nice . . . you're about average.

So there I was, on vacation, standing over a putt on the par 3 third hole at the Alpine Lake golf course in West Virginia, my golfing partner and brother-in-law Don looking on. As I lined up what would undoubtedly be a brilliant putt, a motorist roared past us on an adjacent road and honked his (or her) horn.

I chalked it up to random idiocy, made my putt, and moved on.

The next day, it happened again, this time with Don on the green.

"Must be some kind of local tradition," he joked. I laughed, too, and though we were both a bit annoyed, we played on.

They were just a pair of stupid incidents that marred two otherwise enjoyable days on the course.

Still, the more I thought about them, the more upset I became, and here's why: They're symptoms of a sad, troublesome decay of common courtesy in this country.

Want proof? Read the readers' comments on any website. Listen to elected officials. Check out the talking heads on any of the cable news networks (and I use the word "news" very loosely). Heck, just jump into a car and drive around town. Do any of those things, and it won't be long before your ears are filled with vile, hate-filled vitriol.

When did we become such insufferable bastards? It's as if our ability to spread misery is the only thing that brings us joy. It's toxic. It's poisoning our world. And it's making us sick.

You know what makes us well? Being nice. Really. When you're nice to others, they're usually nice right back. Sometimes they're nice to someone else, too, and *that* person starts being nice. It's contagious.

It works.

Some folks think it's good for the bottom line, too. In their terrific book *The Power of Nice: How to Conquer the Business World with Kindness* (Crown Business, 2006), Linda Kaplan Thaler and Robin Koval claim that "nice companies have lower employee turnover, lower recruitment costs, and higher productivity. Nice people live longer, are healthier, and make more money. In today's interconnected world, companies and people with a reputation for cooperation and fair play forge the kind of relationships that lead to bigger and better opportunities, in business and in life."

Even if they don't do all this, they're just more pleasant to be around. That has to count for *something*, right?

Remember the Golden Rule: "Do unto others as you would have them do unto you." Radical stuff, isn't it? I say we give it a try. We'd be happier, our companies would be more successful, and the world would be a better place.

At the very least, my golf game would improve.

CHAPTER 4
LEARN

Never. Stop. Learning. It's the only way to conquer change and complexity.

It's been said that the most valuable skill we can have in this ever-changing world is the ability to acquire new skills. Success is ours for the taking—we just have to be open to learning new skills, earning new knowledge, asking, listening, absorbing.

Keep your **L > C**—that is, keep your rate of learning ahead of the rate of change.

Piece of cake, right? Actually, yeah. Consider these ideas for doing it.

Doing what's required? You're not doing enough.

"If wishes were horses, beggars would ride."

That's more than a lyrical old English proverb. It's a call to action saying, "Wish all you want, but understand this: No one's going to solve your problems for you. Get off your ass and solve them yourself."

It's obvious that change and complexity are rocking our world and business as usual doesn't cut it anymore. As our friend Emmanuel Gobillot said, "What got you here won't get you there." We need new skills and more knowledge to conquer change.

Jeff Magee is a renowned performance coach and thought leader with the Business Learning Institute. Magee and I talked at length about performance management. He said that it's up to each of us to find those skills and knowledge because "God knows they're not going to find us."

"Successful people are always growing and developing their knowledge set. They're always looking for ways to improve their performance," said Magee. "People who take only the prerequisite forty minimum hours of continuing professional education each year are typically mediocre to mid-level individuals. There is a significant degree of greater success, ability, productivity, and proficiency they can attain individually and organizationally, but they're not pushing themselves to do so."

I know what you're thinking: *Is he really telling us we need to take more CPEs than we're required to?*

In a word, yes.

"The reality is that in today's workplace, we've learned that just being average is acceptable," said Magee. "We've created a society in which everybody points fingers at problems but nobody gets into the game to fix them. The worst part is that we have clients and customers who are paying us to be trusted advisors. They want us to be the plus in the conversation. How can we help someone if we're bringing a minus to the equation?"

Our clients and customers aren't the only ones who benefit. Research has hinted that people devoted to lifelong learning live longer, enjoy better health, have fewer medical problems, and respond more resiliently.

As Magee pointed out, "Benjamin Franklin once said, 'If a man empties his purse into his head, no man can take it away from him. An investment in knowledge always pays the best interest.' You can lose your car, your house, your clothes, but if you have the intellectual capacity to grow and go, you can always bounce back."

Education is broken. Here's one way to fix it.

In his "indispensable" book *Linchpin*, Seth Godin says there are only two things students should be learning in school these days: (1) How to solve interesting problems, and (2) how to lead.

He has a point. Why are our kids devoting so much time and energy memorizing stuff that's readily available via an app or the Internet? Why aren't they spending that time learning something that's really going to set them apart?

As radical as that sounds, Erik Brynjolfsson and Andrew McAfee take Godin's idea even further.

In their riveting 2014 book, *The Second Machine Age: Work, Progress, and Prosperity in a Time of Brilliant Technologies*, Brynjolfsson and McAfee say modern education should focus on just three things:

- Ideation.
- Large-frame pattern recognition.
- Complex communication.

"There's never been a worse time to be a worker with only 'ordinary' skills and abilities to offer," Brynjolfsson and McAfee write, "because computers, robots, and other digital technologies are acquiring these skills and abilities at an extraordinary rate."

In other words, learn stuff that technology isn't going to be able to replace just yet. As awesome as new technology is, it leaves some awfully large gaps in the education landscape. As philosopher Elbert Hubbard once said, "One machine can do the work of 50 ordinary men. No machine can do the work of one extraordinary man."

Our goal, then, is to be extraordinary. Doing so means learning the right things. I wholeheartedly applaud Godin, Brynjolfsson, and McAfee for reimagining education. Our educational system could use a ton of reimagining these days.

For CPAs, though, the answer doesn't have to be that radical.

You still have to know your core technical competencies. Technology hasn't quite been able to replace the accounting, auditing, tax, and finance skills that are the foundation of the profession. Not yet, anyway.

Still, there are new skills you'll need if you want to stand apart from the competition, and these are skills technology will never be able to touch. I'm talking about leadership, innovation, collaboration, social business, and strategic thinking, to name but a few.

This type of training is available now.

Your assumptions are worthless. Ask and learn instead.

I recently closed a long day on the road in an all-too-familiar fashion—by sprinting through Baltimore's airport. I only wanted to get on the plane and fall blissfully asleep.

But when I got to my gate, I was greeted by 110 middle schoolers hopped up on Starbucks and headed back to St. Louis from a field trip to Washington, D.C.

Imagine this: A completely full flight consisting of me, maybe a couple of dozen other business travelers, and 110 highly caffeinated tweens. I don't know what was more priceless—the barely organized chaos of a cross-country field trip or the "God help us" looks on the faces of the rest of us road-weary travelers.

Then the most unexpected thing happened. As Southwest personnel began their pre-boarding announcements, the kids fell silent, moved quietly out of the way, and waited politely for their turn to board. Once on the plane, they were orderly, polite, and extremely well-behaved. With the exception of a few cheers at takeoff and landing, it was as quiet and peaceful as any other flight.

And I felt like an idiot. I was expecting *Animal House* in the sky, and I got *Dead Poets Society* instead.

Lesson learned: Don't assume anything.

- Don't assume the millennial on your team has no loyalty.
- Don't assume your fossil of a boss doesn't "get" social media.
- Don't assume your least-experienced workers don't have any bright ideas.
- Don't assume your leaders have all of the answers.
- Don't assume your employees don't care about learning new things.
- Don't assume you know what your clients/members/employees want.
- Don't assume all of this complexity will go away.

- Don't assume you're too busy to innovate.
- Don't assume you can't change.

Until we ask or experience something, we can't assume anything. Eventually, we'll be proven wrong—as I was on my flight home from Baltimore.

We don't know it all. Every person has something to teach us. We just need to be willing to learn.

Social media in education? It's a natural.

The use of social media is quickly becoming *de rigueur* in almost every corner of corporate America—leadership, marketing, communications, staffing, HR, technology. To varying degrees, people in these areas have embraced blogs, LinkedIn, Facebook, Twitter, and other social media tools—and with good reason. *The social media movement is fundamentally changing the ways in which we communicate and collaborate.*

Lagging a step or three behind, though, is education.

Whether we're talking about college classrooms or CPE programs, most people think of education as a series of one-time live events. The social aspect of education rarely comes to mind, and that's sad because, as Tony Bingham attested in my interview with him, most education is inherently social.

"There's no doubt we have always learned from each other," said Bingham, co-author of *The New Social Learning: A Guide to Transforming Organizations Through Social Media* and CEO of the American Society for Training and Development. "This isn't some new revolutionary concept in learning. What we have now are the tools to accelerate and simplify and document the ways we learn from one another."

I think the problem is that word—*education*. It conjures up images of classrooms and blackboards, textbooks, and No. 2 pencils. The word *learning* is so much more accurate. We wait for others to educate us, but we can *learn* from anything and anyone in any situation.

Social media is merely a tool that enhances our ability to learn.

"Problems are becoming more complex, and typically one person can't solve them efficiently and effectively. You want to leverage the knowledge of many people to do that," Bingham said. "As problems become more complex, you now have the tools that allow groups of people to solve problems. You're not dealing with borders or time constraints. Social media has really opened up the way problem-solving—and, thus, organizational success—can happen in the future."

The CPA profession is a perfect example of that concept, according to Bingham. One thing that differentiates CPAs from others is their ability to solve problems. And these days, new problems are surfacing with unprecedented speed and regularity.

"Going to your peers is a very effective way to learn," said Bingham. "It's a way to stay focused on being the best you can be, by leveraging the best people who are available to solve specific problems. It engages people with each other and gives them resources from which to learn that they might not have had in the past."

In short, education is no longer the exclusive domain of classrooms and professors. Thanks to social media, it can happen anywhere at any time from anyone.

To paraphrase Tom Hood of the Maryland Association of CPAs: *In an era of great change, the most important skill we will possess going forward is the ability to learn new skills.*

And how do we learn? From one another, as Bingham said. Almost everything we learn on a daily basis comes not in a classroom but from our interaction with others. Because social media lets us interact with more people than ever, our ability to learn new skills is greater than ever.

That makes social media an invaluable tool for conquering change.

And e-learning will only grow.

"By 2014, potentially half the workforce will be millennials," Bingham said. "We all know how comfortable they are with social technologies. They are bringing it into the workplace with them. They will be demanding that organizations adopt their approach to learning, and if those organizations don't, they will not be able to attract those workers. Even if they are fortunate enough to attract those workers, they will not be able to retain them and engage them. We're just seeing the beginning of (social learning's) potential impact."

Learn. Share. Repeat.

My daughter Molly had one of those "why do I have to learn this stuff?" episodes on the way home from school recently.

Using math skills she's learned on the way to fourth grade—and without a hint of irony—she said, "I can't believe I have to go to school for twelve more years!"

Partly because parents are required to say stuff like this but mostly because I believe it, I replied, "If you do it right, sweetheart, you'll be learning new stuff for the rest of your life."

That's what I love about CPAs—we get to learn for a living. Most of us struggle to carve out time to learn new stuff, but our designation—our very *careers*—depends on it.

How cool is that?

And yet I still hear instructors complain about folks who come to their CPE programs and hide behind newspapers or laptops for two or four or eight hours. "I don't really want to learn anything," these so-called students are conveying. "Just give me my credits."

Really? In a life this short, you prefer to blow this opportunity to learn something new?

Given the rate of change and complexity these days, you could throw a digital dart at the MACPA's online catalog and find a relevant technical topic you need to learn. Or ditch the technical stuff and brush up on success skills—leadership, sustainability, social media, change management, or personal growth. There's plenty of that to be found through the Business Learning Institute.

Or forget about CPE and learn something *really* radical, like computer programming, or web development, or pretty much anything MIT has to offer. Even places like iTunes U, TED, and the Khan Academy offer fantastic education opportunities—and they're all free.

Look, I don't care what you do. Play guitar. Cook. Needlepoint. Map your family tree. Rewire your house. Create a blog and write a post every day. (Imagine that!)

Just learn something. Then learn something else. Then share it. Don't forget about that part—share what you've learned with others. Help other people learn. (Using social media is a great way of doing that, by the way.)

The point is this: *Always* be learning. Most everything else is a waste of our all-too-short lives.

ACKNOWLEDGMENTS

This isn't my book.

The words are mine but the ideas and inspiration come from the scores of people I've worked with and met over the years. Their wisdom and talent are unmatched. My job is simply to share that wisdom and talent with our members. Without them, this book would not exist.

I'm going to miss somebody, I'm sure. That's the problem with the "Acknowledgments" section: You acknowledge everyone you can think of, then leave someone out and feel like dirt for the rest of forever.

But I'm still going to thank people here because, well, it's what authors do.

So here goes: The folks who made *Look, Lead, Love, Learn* possible, in no particular order:

- To my wife, **Alison**: Thanks for putting up with my late nights on the laptop, and for believing in and supporting all of my social media shenanigans. For all of that and so, so much more . . . I love you.

- To my daughter, **Molly**: If you have read this far, you know Molly is the inspiration for more than a few of these posts. So thanks, sweetheart. Keep that inspiration and attitude coming!

- To **Jackie Brown**: Thanks for believing in me. Letting me telecommute from half a continent away couldn't have been an easy decision, but you never blinked. I'm forever in your debt.

- To the entire **MACPA team**: I couldn't have asked for a better group of colleagues. Your dedication and commitment to CPAs and their profession are unmatched. I'm blessed to be a part of your team.

- To **Tami Bensky**: She was chair of the MACPA Board of Directors in 2007, and CPA Success was her idea. She kicked the

MACPA squarely into the social movement, and we're a better association for it. Thanks for your foresight, Tami!

- To **the thought leaders**: Andrew Zolli, Daniel Burrus, Julie MacIntosh, Peter Sheahan, Geoffrey Moore, Rita McGrath, Emmanuel Gobillot, Brian Solis, Nicole Morris, Tim Sanders, Dave Barry, Laurie's Shoes, the Ritz-Carlton, Southwest Airlines, MBA Airport Transportation, Linda Kaplan Thaler, Robin Koval, Jeff Magee, Tony Bingham, Marcia Connor, et al.—thanks for your inspiring words and ideas. You're changing the world.

- To **Maryland's CPAs, and CPAs every-where**: You're the reason why I do what I do. My goal is to inform you, educate you, make you think—and learn from each and every one of you in the process. Thanks for your integrity, your insight, your foresight, and your dedication to being the world's most trusted business advisors.

- And last but not least, to **Tom Hood**: In Emmanuel Gobillot's words, you make me feel stronger and more capable every day. In my words, you make me want to be better at everything I do. You're an inspiration and a true leader in every sense of the word, and you're the best boss I've ever had. Thanks for everything.

ABOUT THE AUTHOR

Bill Sheridan is a knowledge hunter, content curator, and lifelong learner. As the Maryland Association of CPAs' chief communications officer, editor, and social media cheerleader, he is the creator and co-author of the association's blog, CPA Success. He also writes and produces the MACPA's podcast, CPA Spotlight, and manages the association's numerous social networks.

All of that socializing is paying off. CPA Success has appeared on numerous "top accounting blogs" lists, and Bill's Klout score has earned him the No. 2 spot on SavvySME's list of the top accounting influencers in the world.

Bill speaks regularly to CPAs and association groups on social media and the future of communication, collaboration, and education. Specifically, he has presented at the National Association of

State Boards of Accountancy's 2011 CPE Conference and its 2011 International Conference; the AICPA's inaugural Digital CPA Conference in 2012; and the first-ever CCH Small Firms Conference, also in 2012. He delivers presentations on behalf of the Business Learning Institute and is a certified Insights to Action facilitator.

A journalist by trade, Bill oversees the MACPA's online and print content. His articles about the MACPA and the CPA profession have appeared in the *Journal of Accountancy, Associations Now,* and *SmartCEO.*

Bill is a graduate of the State University of New York at Buffalo. In 2010, he earned the Certified Association Executive designation from the American Society of Association Executives.

Bill is inspired by (and in awe of) his wife, Alison, and their daughter, Molly. They live in St. Louis, Missouri.